The Pity of War

D1644252

The Pity of War
POEMS OF THE FIRST WORLD WAR

selected with an Introduction by
JILL BALCON

Preface by Edward Carpenter
Calligraphy by Rosemary Grossman
Illustrations by Barrington Barber

SHEPHEARD-WALWYN

This edition © Jill Balcon, 1985

First published in this format 1985 by
Shepheard-Walwyn (Publishers) Ltd,
Suite 34, 26 Charing Cross Road,
London WC2H 0DH

ISBN 0 85683 083 6

Printed in Great Britain by Henry Ling Ltd, Dorchester,
on Harrow Matt paper made by St Regis International Ltd
and supplied by Eros Paper Company Ltd.

*In loving memory of Antony Brett-James,
who did not live to complete his years
of work on the First World War.*

Acknowledgements

My gratitude to Iona Opie for her generously given advice and the use of her reference books, and to Alan Martin for his invaluable help throughout.

For permission to include poems of which they control the copyright, grateful acknowledgement is made to the following:

Madame Catherine Guillaume for 'On the March', 'Bombardment' and 'Soliloquy 2'; Mrs. Nicolete Gray and the Society of Authors on behalf of the Laurence Binyon Estate for 'Fetching the Wounded' and 'For the Fallen (September 1914)'; A.D. Peters & Co. Ltd. for 'Festubert: The Old German Line' and '1916 Seen from 1921'; Michael Gibson for 'Mark Anderson' and 'A Lament'; Robert Graves for 'Escape', 'Two Fusiliers', 'A Dedication of Three Hats' and '1915'; Robin Haines, sole trustee of the Gurney Estate 1982 for 'To the Poet before Battle' and 'The First Time In' from *Collected Poems of Ivor Gurney* edited by P.J. Kavanagh (1982) by permission of Oxford University Press; Faber and Faber Ltd. for 'In Parenthesis' by David Jones; William Collins Sons & Co. Ltd. for 'By the Wood' from *Such was my Singing* by Robert Nichols; David Higham Associates Ltd. for 'The Refugees' and 'My Company' from *Collected Poems* by Sir Herbert Read; Mr. George Sassoon for 'Dreamers', 'Attack', 'The Hero', 'The General' and 'Reconciliation' by Siegfried Sassoon.

Contents

Preface

On 11 November 1985, a very evocative date, a memorial was unveiled in Poets' Corner to poets of the First World War, sixteen of whom will be mentioned by name. This is surely timely since there has seldom been such an outpouring of verse. The poets, many of whom were killed in action, left as their legacy imperishable verse wrung out of their own heartache and travail. It is for the reader to decide what their message is and to respond to it as he wills.

I welcome this volume — it could have no more sensitive or perceptive an editor than Jill Balcon — and I am glad to think that in Poets' Corner, Westminster Abbey, we shall be able to remember the war poets, many of whom died before their genius had flowered or were forced into manhood prematurely before the appointed time. If, as one of the most fertile of English authors has written, 'Poets are the trumpets which sing to battle, poets are the unacknolwedged legislators of the world', then maybe countless visitors to Poets' Corner as they look down upon this memorial will think eternal thoughts, pause and consider.

Edward Carpenter
The Deanery, Westminster Abbey 1985

Introduction

The Great War hung over the childhood of my generation, soon to be merged with the foreshadowing of World War II in our early adolescence.

This anthology has been designed to coincide with the placing of a memorial in Westminster Abbey to sixteen poets of the First World War, who wrote during this period and afterwards. My selection was made from the work of these sixteen; the title and subject were dictated by the words of Wilfred Owen on the memorial:

> My subject is War, and the pity of War.
> The Poetry is in the pity.

It so happens that my childhood was largely spent in Westminster, where I was born — a stone's throw from the Abbey. The impact of November 11th on an impressionable child was tremendous. Big Ben struck eleven, and London came to a complete standstill. The men removed their hats, and as the echo died we stood wherever we were for the two minutes' silence. Then we placed a small wooden cross in Abbey Yard. These ritual gestures were not insubstantial. There were the uncles who bore scars, and the photographs of others who had not returned. One of them had joined up at seventeen. There were street musicians, and the legless man who sold sweets by St. James's Park and wore medals. One could not be unaware of ex-servicemen.

In choosing these poems I have tried, as far as possible, to represent different aspects of a harrowing subject. I have not excluded poems that have been in many anthologies. *The Soldier* by Rupert Brooke is an example. I have often said those lines to myself as I walked in those beautifully kept, infinitely moving war cemeteries in France. After two wars there are so many more foreign fields. I have included the whole of *For the Fallen* by Laurence Binyon; I wanted to put into context the lines we hear every Remembrance Day: 'They shall grow not old, as we that are left grow old ...' In his admirable anthology *Men Who March Away* the late I.M.

Parsons, said of David Jones's *In Parenthesis* that 'Extracts divorced from their context lose such a significant degree of force and meaning as to be quite unfair to the work as a whole.' I understand his point of view. In a sense this applies to any extract. But my brief must include a passage from this author, and I am indebted to Tom Durham for generously sharing his knowledge of David Jones's work with me.

Much has been written about Wilfred Owen, whose reputation has been fostered by his three editors — all of them poets themselves — Edmund Blunden, C. Day Lewis, my late husband, and Jon Stallworthy. I hope readers of this book, if they are less familiar with the work of Isaac Rosenberg, will find pleasure in images which linger:

> As I pull the parapet's poppy
> To stick behind my ear

This is the theme of *Reconciliation* too, after the irony and bitterness of Siegfried Sassoon's earlier poems.

I write this in my cottage in Steep, Edward Thomas's village. Fortunately the order of poems is alphabetical to match the memorial stone. Only a fine poet could distil in four lines the essence of all that has gone before. Let him speak the last poignant words and his own epitaph.

Jill Balcon
Steep 1985

ON THE MARCH

Bright berries on the roadside,
Clear among your dusty leaves,
Red mottled berries,
You are beautiful
As the points of a girl's breasts;
You are as firm and fresh.

Beauty of the morning sun
Among the red berries
Of early September,
You tear at my breast,
Your light crushes me
With memory of freedom lost
And warm hours blotted out.

I will throw away rifle and leather belt,
Straps, khaki and heavy nailed boots,
And run naked across the dewy grass
Among the firm red berries!
I will be free
And sing of beauty and the women of Hellas,
Of rent seas and the peace of olive gardens,
Of these rough meadows,

Of the keen welcome smell of London mud!
I will be free. . . .

Party—HALT !

RICHARD ALDINGTON

BOMBARDMENT

Four days the earth was rent and torn
  By bursting steel,
The houses fell about us;
Three nights we dared not sleep,
Sweating, and listening for the imminent crash
Which meant our death.

The fourth night every man,
 Nerve-tortured, racked to exhaustion,
 Slept, muttering and twitching,
 While the shells crashed overhead.

The fifth day there came a hush;
We left our holes
And looked above the wreckage of the earth
To where the white clouds moved in silent lines
Across the untroubled blue.

RICHARD ALDINGTON

3

SOLILOQUY—2

I was wrong, quite wrong;
  The dead men are not always carrion.
After the advance,
As we went through the shattered trenches
Which the enemy had left,
We found, lying upon the fire-step,
A dead English soldier,
His head bloodily bandaged
And his closed left hand touching the earth,

More beautiful than one can tell,
More subtly coloured than a perfect Goya,
And more austere and lovely in repose
Than Angelo's hand could ever carve in stone.

RICHARD ALDINGTON

FETCHING THE WOUNDED

At the road's end glimmer the station lights;
How small beneath the immense hollow of Night's
Lonely and living silence! Air that raced
And tingled on the eyelids as we faced
The long road stretched between the poplars flying
To the dark behind us, shuddering and sighing
With phantom foliage, lapses into hush.
Magical supersession! The loud rush
Swims into quiet: midnight reassumes
Its solitude; there's nothing but great glooms,
Blurred stars; whispering gusts; the hum of wires.
And swerving leftwards upon noiseless tires
We glide over the grass that smells of dew.
A wave of wonder bathes my body through!
For there in the headlamps' gloom-surrounded beam
Tall flowers spring before us, like a dream,
Each luminous little green leaf intimate
And motionless, distinct and delicate
With powdery white bloom fresh upon the stem,
As if that clear beam had created them
Out of darkness. Never so intense
I felt the pang of beauty's innocence,
Earthly and yet unearthly.

A sudden-call!
We leap to ground, and I forget it all.
Each hurries on his errand; lanterns swing;
Dark shapes cross and re-cross the rails; we bring
Stretchers, and pile and number them; and heap
The blankets ready. Then we wait and keep
A listening ear. Nothing comes yet; all's still.
Only soft gusts upon the wires blow shrill
Fitfully, with a gentle spot of rain.
Then, ere one knows it, the long gradual train
Creeps quietly in and slowly stops. No sound
But a few voices' interchange. Around
Is the immense night-stillness, the expanse
Of faint stars over all the wounds of France.

Now stale odour of blood mingles with keen
Pure smell of grass and dew. Now lantern-sheen
Falls on brown faces opening patient eyes
And lips of gentle answers, where each lies
Supine upon his stretcher, black of beard
Or with young cheeks; on caps and tunics smeared
And stained, white bandages round foot or head
Or arm, discoloured here and there with red.
Sons of all corners of wide France; from Lille,
Douay, the land beneath the invader's heel,

Champagne, Touraine, the fisher-villages
Of Brittany, the valleyed Pyrenees,
Blue coasts of the South, old Paris streets. Argonne
Of ever smouldering battle, that anon
Leaps furious, brothered them in arms. They fell
In the trenched forest scarred with reeking shell.
Now strange the sound comes round them in the night
Of English voices. By the wavering light
Quickly we have borne them, one by one, to the air,
And sweating in the dark lift up with care,
Tense-sinewed, each to his place. The cars at last
Complete their burden: slowly, and then fast
We glide away.
     And the dim round of sky,
Infinite and silent, broods unseeingly
Over the shadowy uplands rolling black
Into far woods, and the long road we track
Bordered with apparitions, as we pass,
Of trembling poplars and lamp-whitened grass,
A brief procession flitting like a thought
Through a brain drowsing into slumber; nought
But we awake in the solitude immense!
But hurting the vague dumbess of my sense
Are fancies wandering the night: there steals
Into my heart, like something that one feels

In darkness, the still presence of far homes
Lost in deep country, and in little rooms
The vacant bed. I touch the world of pain
That is so silent. Then I see again
Only those infinitely patient faces
In the lantern beam, beneath the night's vast spaces,
Amid the shadows and the scented dew;
And those illumined flowers, springing anew
In freshness like a smile of secrecy
From the gloom-buried earth, return to me.
The village sleeps; blank walls, and windows barred.
But lights are moving in the hushed courtyard
As we glide up to the open door. The Chief
Gives every man his order, prompt and brief.
We carry up our wounded, one by one.
The first cock crows: the morrow is begun.

LAURENCE BINYON

FOR THE FALLEN (September 1914)

With proud thanksgiving, a mother for her children,
England mourns for her dead across the sea.
Flesh of her flesh they were, spirit of her spirit,
Fallen in the cause of the free.

Solemn the drums thrill: Death august and royal
Sings sorrow up into immortal spheres.
There is music in the midst of desolation
And a glory that shines upon our tears.

They went with songs to the battle, they were young,
Straight of limb, true of eye, steady and aglow.
They were staunch to the end against odds uncounted,
They fell with their faces to the foe.

They shall not grow old, as we that are left grow old:
Age shall not weary them, nor the years condemn.
At the going down of the sun and in the morning
We will remember them.

They mingle not with their laughing comrades again;
They sit no more at familiar tables of home;
They have no lot in our labour of the day-time;
They sleep beyond England's foam.

But where our desires are and our hopes profound,
Felt as a well-spring that is hidden from sight,
To the innermost heart of their own land they are known
As the stars are known to the Night.

As the stars that shall be bright when we are dust,
Moving in marches upon the heavenly plain,
As the stars that are starry in the time of our darkness,
To the end, to the end, they remain.

LAURENCE BINYON

FESTUBERT: THE OLD GERMAN LINE

Sparse mists of moonlight hurt our eyes
  With gouged and scourged uncertainties
Of soul and soil in agonies.

One derelict grim skeleton
That drench and dry had battened on
Still seemed to wish us malison;

Still zipped across the gouts of lead
Or cracked like whipcracks overhead;
The gray rags fluttered on the dead.

EDMUND BLUNDEN

1916 seen from 1921

Tired with dull grief, grown old before my day,
  I sit in solitude and only hear
Long silent laughters, murmurings of dismay,
The lost intensities of hope and fear;
In those old marshes yet the rifles lie,
On the thin breastwork flutter the grey rags,
The very books I read are there—and I
Dead as the men I loved, wait while life drags

Its wounded length from those sad streets of war
Into green places here, that were my own;
But now what once was mine is mine no more,
I seek such neighbours here and I find none.
With such strong gentleness and tireless will
Those ruined houses seared themselves in me,
Passionate I look for their dumb story still,
And the charred stub outspeaks the living tree.

I rise up at the singing of a bird
And scarcely knowing slink along the lane,
I dare not give a soul a look or word
Where all have homes and none's at home in vain:
Deep red the rose burned in the grim redoubt,
The self-sown wheat around was like a flood,
In the hot path the lizard lolled time out,
The saints in broken shrines were bright as blood.

Sweet Mary's shrine between the sycamores!
There we would go, my friend of friends and I,
And snatch long moments from the grudging wars,
Whose dark made light intense to see them by.
Shrewd bit the morning fog, the whining shots
Spun from the wrangling wire; then in warm swoon
The sun hushed all but the cool orchard plots,
We crept in the tall grass and slept till noon.

EDMUND BLUNDEN

13

THE SOLDIER

If I should die, think only this of me:
  That there's some corner of a foreign field
That is for ever England. There shall be
  In that rich earth a richer dust concealed;
A dust whom England bore, shaped, made aware,
  Gave, once, her flowers to love, her ways to roam,
A body of England's, breathing English air,
  Washed by the rivers, blest by suns of home.

And think, this heart, all evil shed away,
  A pulse in the eternal mind, no less
    Gives somewhere back the thoughts by England given;
Her sights and sounds; dreams happy as her day;
  And laughter, learnt of friends; and gentleness,
    In hearts at peace, under an English heaven.

RUPERT BROOKE

THE DEAD

These hearts were woven of human joys and cares,
  Washed marvellously with sorrow, swift to mirth.
The years had given them kindness. Dawn was theirs,
    And sunset, and the colours of the earth.
These had seen movement, and heard music; known
    Slumber and waking; loved; gone proudly friended;
Felt the quick stir of wonder; sat alone;
    Touched flowers and furs and cheeks. All this is ended.

There are waters blown by changing winds to laughter
And lit by the rich skies, all day. And after,
    Frost, with a gesture, stays the waves that dance
And wandering loveliness. He leaves a white
    Unbroken glory, a gathered radiance,
A width, a shining peace, under the night.

RUPERT BROOKE

MARK ANDERSON

On the low table by the bed
  Where it was set aside last night,
Beyond the bandaged lifeless head,
It glitters in the morning light—

And as the hours of morning pass
I cannot sleep, I cannot think,
But only gaze upon the glass
Of water that he could not drink.

WILFRID WILSON GIBSON

A LAMENT

We who are left, how shall we look again
    Happily on the sun, or feel the rain,
Without remembering how they who went
Ungrudgingly, and spent
Their all for us, loved, too, the sun and rain?

A bird among the rain-wet lilac sings—
But we, how shall we turn to little things
And listen to the birds and winds and streams
Made holy by their dreams,
Nor feel the heart-break in the heart of things?

WILFRID WILSON GIBSON

1915

I've watched the Seasons passing slow, so slow,
In the fields between La Bassée and Béthune;
Primroses and the first warm day of Spring,
Red poppy floods of June,
August, and yellowing Autumn, so
To Winter nights knee-deep in mud or snow,
And you've been everything,

Dear, you've been everything that I most lack
In these soul-deadening trenches – pictures, books,
Music, the quiet of an English wood,
Beautiful comrade-looks,
The narrow, bouldered mountain-track,
The broad, full-bosomed ocean, green and black,
And Peace, and all that's good.

ROBERT GRAVES

ESCAPE

(August 6th 1916. — Officer previously reported
died of wounds, now reported wounded.
Graves, Captain R., Royal Welch Fusiliers.)

     But I *was* dead, an hour or more.
. . . I woke when I'd already passed the door
That Cerberus guards, and half-way down the road
To Lethe, as an old Greek signpost showed.
Above me, on my stretcher swinging by,
I saw new stars in the subterrene sky:
A Cross, a Rose in bloom, a Cage with bars,
And a barbed Arrow feathered in fine stars.
I felt the vapours of forgetfulness
Float in my nostrils. Oh, may Heaven bless
Dear Lady Proserpine, who saw me wake,
And, stooping over me, for Henna's sake
Cleared my poor buzzing head and sent me back
Breathless, with leaping heart along the track.

After me roared and clattered angry hosts
Of demons, heroes, and policeman-ghosts.
"Life! life! I can't be dead! I won't be dead!
Damned if I'll die for anyone!" I said....
Cerberus stands and grins above me now,
Wearing three heads—lion and lynx, and sow.
Quick, a revolver! But my Webley's gone,
Stolen... No bombs... no knife...The crowd
    swarms on,
Bellows, hurls stones. ...Not even a honeyed sop...
Nothing. ...Good Cerberus!...Good dog!...
    but stop!
Stay...A great luminous thought...I do believe
There's still some morphia that I bought on leave.
Then swiftly Cerberus' wide mouths I cram
With army biscuit smeared with ration jam;
And sleep lurks in the luscious plum and apple.
He crunches, swallows, stiffens, seems to grapple
With the all-powerful poppy....then a snore,
A crash; the beast blocks up the corridor
With monstrous hairy carcase, red and dun—
Too late! for I've sped through.
                    O Life! O Sun!

ROBERT GRAVES

TWO FUSILIERS

And have we done with War at last?
 Well, we've been lucky devils both,
And there's no need of pledge or oath
To bind our lovely friendship fast,
By firmer stuff
Close bound enough.

By wire and wood and stake we're bound,
By Fricourt and by Festubert,
By whipping rain, by the sun's glare,
By all the misery and loud sound,
By a Spring day,
By Picard clay.

Show me the two so closely bound
As we, by the wet bond of blood,
By friendship blossoming from mud,
By Death: we faced him, and we found
Beauty in Death,
In dead men, breath.

ROBERT GRAVES

A DEDICATION OF THREE HATS

This round hat I devote to Mars,
  Tough steel with leather lined.
My skin's my own, redeemed by scars
From further still more futile wars
The god may have in mind.

Minerva takes my square of black
Well tasselled with the same;
Her dullest nurselings never lack
With hoods of scarlet at their back
And letters to their name.

But this third hat, the foolscap sheet,
(For there's a strength in three)
Unblemished, conical and neat
I hang up here without deceit
To kind Euphrosyne.

Goddess, accept with smiles or tears
This gift of a gross fool
Who having sweated in death fears
With wounds and cramps for three long years
Limped back, and sat for school.

ROBERT GRAVES

INTO BATTLE (Flanders, April 1915)

The naked earth is warm with Spring,
  And with green grass and bursting trees
Leans to the sun's gaze glorying,
  And quivers in the sunny breeze;

And life is colour and warmth and light,
  And a striving evermore for these;
And he is dead who will not fight;
  And who dies fighting has increase.

The fighting man shall from the sun
   Take warmth, and life from the glowing earth;
Speed with the light-foot winds to run,
   And with the trees to newer birth;
And find, when fighting shall be done,
   Great rest, and fullness after dearth.

All the bright company of Heaven
   Hold him in their high comradeship,
The Dog-Star, and the Sisters Seven,
   Orion's Belt and sworded hip.

The woodland trees that stand together,
   They stand to him each one a friend;
They gently speak in the windy weather;
   They guide to valley and ridge's end.

The kestrel hovering by day,
   And the little owls that call by night,
Bid him be swift and keen as they,
   As keen of ear, as swift of sight.

The blackbird sings to him, 'Brother, brother,
   If this be the last song you shall sing,
Sing well, for you may not sing another;
   Brother, sing.'

In dreary, doubtful waiting hours,
    Before the brazen frenzy starts,
The horses show him nobler powers;
    O patient eyes, courageous hearts!

And when the burning moment breaks,
    And all things else are out of mind,
And only joy of battle takes
    Him by the throat, and makes him blind,

Through joy and blindness he shall know,
    Not caring much to know, that still
Nor lead nor steel shall reach him, so
    That it be not the Destined Will.

The thundering line of battle stands,
    And in the air Death moans and sings;
But Day shall clasp him with strong hands,
    And Night shall fold him in soft wings.

JULIAN GRENFELL

TO THE POET BEFORE BATTLE

Now, youth, the hour of thy dread passion comes;
Thy lovely things must all be laid away;
And thou, as others, must face the riven day
Unstirred by rattle of the rolling drums,
Or bugles' strident cry. When mere noise numbs
The sense of being, the fear-sick soul doth sway,
Remember thy great craft's honour, that they may say
Nothing in shame of poets. Then the crumbs
Of praise the little versemen joyed to take
Shall be forgotten; then they must know we are,
For all our skill in words, equal in might
And strong of mettle as those we honoured; make
The name of poet terrible in just war,
And like a crown of honour upon the fight.

IVOR GURNEY

FIRST TIME IN

After the dread tales and red yarns of the Line
  Anything might have come to us; but the divine
Afterglow brought us up to a Welsh colony
Hiding in sandbag ditches, whispering consolatory
Soft foreign things. Then we were taken in
To low huts candle-lit, shaded close by slitten
Oilsheets, and there the boys gave us kind welcome,
So that we looked out as from the edge of home.
Sang us Welsh things, and changed all former notions
To human hopeful things. And the next day's guns
Nor any line-pangs ever quite could blot out
That strangely beautiful entry to war's rout;
Candles they gave us, precious and shared over-rations—
Ulysses found little more in his wanderings without doubt.
'David of the White Rock', the 'Slumber Song' so soft, and that
Beautiful tune to which roguish words by Welsh pit boys
Are sung–but never more beautiful than there
                    under the guns' noise.

IVOR GURNEY

IN PARENTHESIS
From Part 3 – The Rat of No-man's-land.

You can hear the silence of it:
you can hear the rat of no-man's-land
rut-out intricacies,
weasel-out his patient workings,
scrut, scrut, sscrut,
harrow out-earthly, trowel his cunning paw;
redeem the time of our uncharity, to sap his own
amphibious paradise.
   You can hear his carrying-parties rustle our corruptions
through the night-weeds–contest the choicest morsels in his
tiny conduits, bead-eyed feast on us; by a rule of his nature,
at night-feast on the broken of us.
   Those broad-pinioned; [1]
blue-burnished, or brinded-back;
whose proud eyes watched
                    the broken emblems
droop and drag dust,
suffer with us this metamorphosis.
   These too have shed their fine feathers; these too have
slimed their dark-bright coats; these too have condescended
to dig in.

1. *Cf.* Anglo-Saxon poem 'The Battle of Brunanbush'.

The white-tailed eagle at the battle ebb, 2
                    where the sea wars against the river,
the speckled kite of Maldon
and the crow
have naturally selected to be un-winged;
to go on the belly, to
sap   sap   sap
with festered spines, arched under the moon; furrit
with whiskered snouts the secret parts of us.
  When it's all quiet you can hear them:
scrut scrut scrut
when it's as quiet as this is.
  It's so very still.
  Your body fits the crevice of the bay in the most
comfortable fashion imaginable.
  It's cushy enough.

  The relief elbows him on the fire-step: All quiet china?
—bugger all to report?—kipping mate?—christ, mate—
you'll 'ave 'em all over.

2. *Cf.* Dafydd Benfras (13th century) *Elegy to the Sons of Llewelyn the Great.*

From Part 4— Daily Rations at the Front.

In a little while they came again, the Lance-Corporal
with his file of two, carrying a full sack.
   No.1 section gathered, bunched, in the confined traverse;
that lance-jack balances carefully his half mess-tin of rum.
   They bring for them,
in common:
Loose tea mingled with white sugar, tied in heel of
sandbag, pudding fashion, congealed, clinging to
the hemp mesh, and one tin of butter.
   They bring for them,
for each and for several;
he makes division, he ordains:
three ration biscuits,
one-third part of a loaf,
two Field Service postcards,
one Field Service envelope,
one piece of cheese of uncertain dimension, clammy,
pitted with earth and very hairy, imprinted with the
sodden hessian's weft and warp; powerfully unappetising;
one tin of Tickler's plum and apple for three,
two packets of Trumpeter for cigarette smokers,
one tin of issue tobacco for pipe smokers.
   They press forward, they speak half audibly or stand aloof. [3]

3. By far the greater number of men smoked cigarettes rather than pipes, and those who did complained
bitterly of the particular blend of ration tobacco, so that the issuing of these things usually called for
considerable tact on the part of the N.C.O. in charge, and strained the amiability of those among whom
they were divided.

Their mixed round-skulls, long-barrow heads, nobble each.
Stratford-atte-Bowe mingles west-tribe modulated high and
low in their complaint.

DAVID JONES

BY THE WOOD

How still the day is, and the air how bright!
  A thrush sings and is silent in the wood;
The hillside sleeps dizzy with heat and light;
A rhythmic murmur fills the quietude;
A woodpecker prolongs his leisured flight,
Rising and falling on the solitude.

But there are those who far from yon wood lie,
Buried within the trench where all were found.
A weight of mould oppresses every eye,
Within that cabin close their limbs are bound,
And there they rot amid the long profound,
Disastrous silence of grey earth and sky.

These once, too, rested where now rests but one,
Who scarce can lift his panged and heavy head,
Who drinks in grief the hot light of the sun,
Whose eyes watch dully the green branches spread,
Who feels his currents ever a slowlier run,
Whose lips repeat a silent '...Dead! all dead!'

O youths to come shall drink air warm and bright,
Shall hear the bird cry in the sunny wood,
All my Young England fell today in fight:
That bird, that wood, was ransomed by our blood!

I pray you when the drum rolls let your mood
Be worthy of our deaths and your delight.

ROBERT NICHOLS

THE SEND-OFF

Down the close darkening lanes they sang their way
To the siding-shed,
And lined the train with faces grimly gay.

Their breasts were stuck all white with wreath and spray
As men's are, dead.

Dull porters watched them, and a casual tramp
Stood staring hard,
Sorry to miss them from the upland camp.

Then, unmoved, signals nodded, and a lamp
Winked to the guard.

So secretly, like wrongs hushed-up, they went.
They were not ours:
We never heard to which front these were sent;

Nor there if they yet mock what women meant
Who gave them flowers.

Shall they return to beatings of great bells
In wild train-loads?
A few, a few, too few for drums and yells,

May creep back, silent, to village wells,
Up half-known roads.

WILFRED OWEN

ANTHEM FOR DOOMED YOUTH

What passing-bells for these who die as cattle?
   —Only the monstrous anger of the guns.
      Only the stuttering rifles' rapid rattle
Can patter out their hasty orisons.
No mockeries now for them; no prayers nor bells;
      Nor any voice of mourning save the choirs,—
The shrill, demented choirs of wailing shells;
      And bugles calling for them from sad shires.

What candles may be held to speed them all?
      Not in the hands of boys, but in their eyes
Shall shine the holy glimmers of goodbyes.
      The pallor of girls' brows shall be their pall;
Their flowers the tenderness of patient minds,
And each slow dusk a drawing-down of blinds.

WILFRED OWEN

STRANGE MEETING

It seemed that out of battle I escaped
Down some profound dull tunnel, long since scooped
Through granites which titanic wars had groined.

Yet also there encumbered sleepers groaned,
Too fast in thought or death to be bestirred.
Then, as I probed them, one sprang up, and stared
With piteous recognition in fixed eyes,
Lifting distressful hands as if to bless.
And by his smile, I knew that sullen hall —
By his dead smile I knew we stood in Hell.

With a thousand pains that vision's face was grained;
Yet no blood reached there from the upper ground,
And no guns thumped, or down the flues made moan.
'Strange friend,' I said, 'here is no cause to mourn.'
'None,' said that other, 'save the undone years,
The hopelessness. Whatever hope is yours,
Was my life also; I went hunting wild
After the wildest beauty in the world,
Which lies not calm in eyes, or braided hair,
But mocks the steady running of the hour,
And if it grieves, grieves richlier than here.

For by my glee might many men have laughed,
And of my weeping something had been left,
Which must die now. I mean the truth untold,
The pity of war, the pity war distilled.
Now men will go content with what we spoiled,
Or, discontent, boil bloody, and be spilled.
They will be swift with swiftness of the tigress.
None will break ranks, though nations trek from progres.
Courage was mine, and I had mystery,
Wisdom was mine, and I had mastery:
To miss the march of this retreating world
Into vain citadels that are not walled.
Then, when much blood had clogged their chariot-whee
I would go up and wash them from sweet wells,
Even with truths that lie too deep for taint.
I would have poured my spirit without stint
But not through wounds; not on the cess of war.
Foreheads of men have bled where no wounds were.

'I am the enemy you killed, my friend.
I knew you in this dark: for so you frowned
Yesterday through me as you jabbed and killed.
I parried; but my hands were loath and cold.
Let us sleep now. . . .'

WILFRED OWEN

38

FUTILITY

Move him into the sun –
  Gently its touch awoke him once,
At home, whispering of fields unsown.
Always it woke him, even in France,
Until this morning and this snow.
If anything might rouse him now
The kind old sun will know.

Think how it wakes the seeds,—
Woke, once, the clays of a cold star.
Are limbs, so dear-achieved, are sides,
Full-nerved– still warm– too hard to stir?
Was it for this the clay grew tall?
— O what made fatuous sunbeams toil
To break earth's sleep at all?

WILFRED OWEN

THE REFUGEES

Mute figures with bowed heads
    They travel along the road:
Old women, incredibly old,
And a hand-cart of chattels.

They do not weep:
Their eyes are too raw for tears.

Past them have hastened
Processions of retreating gunteams,
Baggage-wagons and swift horsemen.
Now they struggle along
With the rearguard of a broken army.

We will hold the enemy towards nightfall
And they will move
Mutely into the dark behind us,
Only the creaking cart
Disturbing their sorrowful serenity.

HERBERT READ

MY COMPANY

Foule! Ton âme entière est debout dans mon corps.

Jules Romains.

1.

You became
In many acts and quiet observances
A body and a soul, entire.

I cannot tell
What time your life became mine:
Perhaps when one summer night
We halted on the roadside
In the starlight only,
And you sang your sad home-songs,
Dirges which I standing outside you
Coldly condemned.

Perhaps, one night, descending cold
When rum was mighty acceptable,
And my doling gave birth to sensual gratitude.

And then our fights: we've fought together
Compact, unanimous;
And I have felt the pride of leadership.

In many acts and quiet observances
You absorbed me:
Until one day I stood eminent
And saw you gathered round me,
Uplooking,
And about you a radiance that seemed to beat
With variant glow and to give
Grace to our unity.

But, God! I know that I'll stand
Someday in the loneliest wilderness,
Someday my heart will cry
For the soul that has been, but that now
Is scattered with the winds,
Deceased and devoid.

I know that I'll wander with a cry:
"O beautiful men, O men I loved,
O whither are you gone, my company?"

2.

My men go wearily
With their monstrous burdens.

They bear wooden planks
And iron sheeting
Through the area of death.

When a flare curves through the sky
They rest immobile.

Then on again,
Sweating and blaspheming—
"Oh, bloody Christ!"

My men, my modern Christs,
Your bloody agony confronts the world.

3.

A man of mine
        lies on the wire.
It is death to fetch his soulless corpse.

A man of mine
        lies on the wire;
And he will rot
And first his lips
The worms will eat.

It is not thus I would have him kissed,
But with the warm passionate lips
Of his comrade here.

4.

I can assume
A giant attitude and godlike mood,
And then detachedly regard
All riots, conflicts and collisions.

The men I've lived with
Lurch suddenly into a far perspective;
They distantly gather like a dark cloud of birds
In the autumn sky.

Urged by some unanimous
Volition or fate,
Clouds clash in opposition;
The sky quivers, the dead descend;
Earth yawns.

They are all of one species.

From my giant attitude,
In godlike mood,

I laugh till space is filled
With hellish merriment.

Then again I assume
My human docility,
Bow my head
And share their doom.

HERBERT READ

RETURNING, WE HEAR THE LARKS

Sombre the night is.
And though we have our lives, we know
What sinister threat lurks there.

Dragging these anguished limbs, we only know
This poison-blasted track opens on our camp—
On a little safe sleep.

But hark! joy—joy—strange joy.
Lo! heights of night ringing with unseen larks.
Music showering on our upturned list'ning faces.

Death could drop from the dark
As easily as song—
But song only dropped,
Like a blind man's dreams on the sand
By dangerous tides,
Like a girl's dark hair for she dreams no
    ruin lies there,
Or her kisses where a serpent hides.

ISAAC ROSENBERG

BREAK OF DAY IN THE TRENCHES

The darkness crumbles away—
  It is the same old druid Time as ever.
Only a live thing leaps my hand—
A queer sardonic rat—
As I pull the parapet's poppy
To stick behind my ear.
Droll rat, they would shoot you if they knew
Your cosmopolitan sypathies.
Now you have touched this English hand
You will do the same to a German—
Soon, no doubt, if it be your pleasure
To cross the sleeping green between.
It seems you inwardly grin as you pass
Strong eyes, fine limbs, haughty athletes
Less chanced than you for life,
Bonds to the whims of murder,
Sprawled in the bowels of the earth,
The torn fields of France.
What do you see in our eyes
At the shrieking iron and flame
 Hurled through still heavens?
What quaver—what heart aghast?

Poppies whose roots are in man's veins
Drop, and are ever dropping;
But mine in my ear is safe,
Just a little white with the dust.

ISAAC ROSENBERG

DREAMERS

Soldiers are citizens of death's grey land,
    Drawing no dividend from time's to-morrows.
In the great hour of destiny they stand,
Each with his feuds, and jealousies, and sorrows.
Soldiers are sworn to action; they must win
Some flaming, fatal climax with their lives.
Soldiers are dreamers; when the guns begin
They think of firelit homes, clean beds and wives.

I see them in foul dug-outs, gnawed by rats,
And in the ruined trenches, lashed with rain,
Dreaming of things they did with balls and bats,
And mocked by hopeless longing to regain
Bank-holidays, and picture shows, and spats,
And going to the office in the train.

SIEGFRIED SASSOON

ATTACK

At dawn the ridge emerges massed and dun
In the wild purple of the glow'ring sun,
Smouldering through spouts of drifting smoke
   that shroud
The menacing scarred slope; and, one by one,
Tanks creep and topple forward to the wire.
The barrage roars and lifts. Then, clumsily bowed
With bombs and guns and shovels and battle-gear,
Men jostle and climb to meet the bristling fire.
Lines of grey, muttering faces, masked with fear,
They leave their trenches, going over the top,
While time ticks blank and busy on their wrists,
And hope, with furtive eyes and grappling fists,
Flounders in mud. O Jesus, make it stop!

SIEGFRIED SASSOON

51

THE HERO

'Jack fell as he'd have wished,' the Mother said,
  And folded up the letter that she'd read.
'The Colonel writes so nicely.' Something broke
In the tired voice that quavered to a choke.
She half looked up. 'We mothers are so proud
Of our dead soldiers.' Then her face was bowed.

Quietly the Brother Officer went out.
He'd told the poor old dear some gallant lies
That she would nourish all her days, no doubt.
For while he coughed and mumbled, her weak eyes
Had shone with gentle triumph, brimmed with joy,
Because he'd been so brave, her glorious boy.

He thought how 'Jack', cold-footed, useless swine,
Had panicked down the trench that night the mine
Went up at Wicked Corner; how he'd tried
To get sent home, and how, at last, he died,
Blown to small bits. And no one seemed to care
Except that lonely woman with white hair.

SIEGFRIED SASSOON

THE GENERAL

'Good-morning; good-morning!' the General said
When we met him last week on our way to the line.
Now the soldiers he smiled at are most of 'em dead,
And we're cursing his staff for incompetent swine.
'He's a cheery old card,' grunted Harry to Jack
As they slogged up to Arras with rifle and pack.
. . . .
And he did for them both by his plan of attack.

SIEGFRIED SASSOON

RECONCILIATION

When you are standing at your hero's grave,
Or near some homeless village where he died,
Remember, through your heart's rekindling pride,
The German soldiers who were loyal and brave.

Men fought like brutes; and hideous things were done;
And you have nourished hatred, harsh and blind.
But in that Golgotha perhaps you'll find
The mothers of the men who killed your son.

November 1918.

SIEGFRIED SASSOON

'ALL THE HILLS AND VALES ALONG'

All the hills and vales along
    Earth is bursting into song,
And the singers are the chaps
Who are going to die perhaps.
    O sing, marching men,
    Till the valleys ring again.
    Give your gladness to earth's keeping,
    So be glad, when you are sleeping.

Cast away regret and rue,
Think what you are marching to.
Little live, great pass.
Jesus Christ and Barabbas
Were found the same day.
This died, that went his way.
    So sing with joyful breath,
    For why, you are going to death.
    Teeming earth will surely store
    All the gladness that you pour.

Earth that never doubts nor fears,
Earth that knows of death, not tears,
Earth that bore with joyful ease
Hemlock for Socrates,
Earth that blossomed and was glad
'Neath the cross that Christ had,
Shall rejoice and blossom too
When the bullet reaches you.
    Wherefore, men marching
    On the road to death, sing!
    Pour your gladness on earth's head,
    So be merry, so be dead.

From the hills and valleys earth
Shouts back the sound of mirth,
Tramp of feet and lilt of song
Ringing all the road along.
All the music of their going,
Ringing swinging glad song-throwing,
Earth will echo still, when foot
Lies numb and voice mute.
    On, marching men, on
    To the gates of death with song.
    Sow your gladness for earth's reaping,
    So you may be glad, though sleeping.

Strew your gladness on earth's bed,
So be merry, so be dead.

CHARLES SORLEY

TWO SONNETS (12th June 1915)

I

Saints have adored the lofty soul of you.
Poets have whitened at your high renown.
We stand among the many millions who
Do hourly wait to pass your pathway down.
You, so familiar, once were strange: we tried
To live as of your presence unaware.
But now in every road on every side
We see your straight and steadfast signpost there.

I think it like that signpost in my land,
Hoary and tall, which pointed me to go
Upward, into the hills, on the right hand,
Where the mists swim and winds shriek and blow,
A homeless land and friendless, but a land
I did not know and that I wished to know.

II

Such, such is Death: no triumph: no defeat:
  Only an empty pail, a slate rubbed clean,
A merciful putting away of what has been.

And this we know: Death is not Life effete,
Life crushed, the broken pail. We who have seen
So marvelous things know well the end not yet.

Victor and vanquished are a-one in death:
Coward and brave: friend, foe. Ghosts do not say
'Come, what was your record when you drew breath?'
But a big blot has hid each yesterday
So poor, so manifestly incomplete.
And your bright Promise, withered long and sped,
Is touched, stirs, rises, opens and grows sweet
And blossoms and is you, when you are dead.

CHARLES SORLEY

A PRIVATE

This ploughman dead in battle slept out of doors
  Many a frozen night, and merrily
Answered staid drinkers, good bedmen, and all
    bores:
"At Mrs. Greenland's Hawthorn Bush," said he,
"I slept." None knew which bush. Above the town,
Beyond "The Drover," a hundred spot the down
In Wiltshire. And where now at last he sleeps
More sound in France—that, too, he secret keeps.

EDWARD THOMAS

60

ROADS

I love roads:
  The goddesses that dwell
Far along them invisible
Are my favourite gods.

Roads go on
While we forget, and are
Forgotten like a star
That shoots and is gone.

On this earth 'tis sure
We men have not made
Anything that doth fade
So soon, so long endure:

The hill road wet with rain
In the sun would not gleam
Like a winding stream
If we trod it not again.

They are lonely
While we sleep, lonelier
For lack of the traveller
Who is now a dream only.

From dawn's twilight
And all the clouds like sheep
On the mountains of sleep
They wind into the night.

The next turn may reveal
Heaven: upon the crest
The close pine clump, at rest
And black, may Hell conceal.

Often footsore, never
Yet of the road I weary,
Though long and steep and dreary,
As it winds on for ever.

Helen of the roads,
The mountain ways of Wales
And the Mabinogion tales
Is one of the true gods,

Abiding in the trees,
The threes and fours so wise,
The larger companies,
That by the roadside be,

And beneath the rafter
Else uninhabited
Excepting by the dead;
And it is her laughter

At morn and night I hear
When the thrush cock sings
Bright irrelevant things,
And when the chanticleer

Calls back to their own night
Troops that make loneliness
With their light footsteps' press,
As Helen's own are light.

Now all roads lead to France
And heavy is the tread
Of the living; but the dead
Returning lightly dance:

Whatever the road bring
To me or take from me,
They keep me company
With their pattering,

Crowding the solitude
Of the loops over the downs,
Hushing the roar of towns
And their brief multitude.

EDWARD THOMAS

LIGHTS OUT

I have come to the borders of sleep,
The unfathomable deep
Forest where all must lose
Their way, however straight,
Or winding, soon or late;
They cannot choose.

Many a road and track
That, since the dawn's first crack,
Up to the forest brink,
Deceived the travellers,
Suddenly now blurs,
And in they sink.

Here love ends—
Despair, ambition ends:
All pleasure and all trouble,
Although most sweet or bitter,
Here ends in sleep that is sweeter
Than tasks most noble.

There is not any book
Or face of dearest look
That I would not turn from now
To go into the unknown
I must enter, and leave, alone,
I know not how.

The tall forest towers;
Its cloudy foliage lowers
Ahead, shelf above shelf;
Its silence I hear and obey
That I may lose my way
And myself.

EDWARD THOMAS

IN MEMORIAM (Easter 1915)

The flowers left thick at nightfall in the wood
This Eastertide call into mind the men,
Now far from home, who, with their sweethearts, should
Have gathered them and will do never again.

EDWARD THOMAS

Index of First Lines